REDEEMED TALK

By: Dr. H. L. "Skip" Horton, Apostle

FOREWORD

Let the words of my mouth. . .

Redeemed Talk is a collection of "Spiritual-Awareness" phrases that is designed to teach, preach and edify those who are seeking a closer relationship with God. This book is divided into three major categories to classify each phrase according to its significance. One phrase or more may be classified under one category or another.

We are living in a day where people are dull of hearing. There are so many distractions coming our way. The enemy is filling our minds with undesirable thoughts, unnecessary thoughts, fantasy thoughts, lying thoughts and depressing thoughts. Isaiah said, *"When the enemy comes in like a flood, the Spirit of the Lord shall lift up a standard against him."*

This on-going collection of sayings, spoken to the Body of Christ by Apostle Horton is to edify God and remind us to focus on Him. It is not what you say, it's what you keep saying that people remember! Apostle Horton has continually spoken words of encouragement given to him by the Holy Spirit.

Redeemed Talk will teach us the principles of God, and it also will teach us how to call into existence those principles. Journey through this collection of thoughts and spiritual insightfulness, aimed at removing from our mind and mouth negative words to propel us into Redeemed Talk.

As you read this book, may you be encouraged, inspired, and most of all, may your mind be **RENEWED!**

WORDS

ARE

THOUGHTS

AND

THOUGHTS

ARE

THINGS

"Now faith is the substance of things hoped for, the evidence of things not seen. For by it the elders obtained a good report. Through faith we understand that the worlds were framed by the word of God, so that things which are seen were not made of things which do appear."
Hebrews 11:1, 2, 3

TABLE OF CONTENTS
REDEEMED TALK

" . . . the words that I speak unto you,
they are spirit, and they are life."
John 6:63

"SPEAKING WITH AUTHORITY"

By
Dr. H. L. "Skip" Horton, Apostle
The Day Star Tabernacle International
8200 Hwy. 166
Douglasville, GA 30135
(770) 949-LOVE

**"Let the redeemed of the Lord say so,
whom he hath redeemed from the
hand of the enemy."**
Psalm 107:2

ABOUT THE AUTHOR

Dr. H. L. "Skip" Horton, Apostle
THE DAY STAR TABERNACLE
INTERNATIONAL

God gave the man of God a vision to teach the whole Bible without denominational persuasion with the zeal of God performing the vision. In 1984, God honored Dr. Horton with a vision, and The Bright Star Church was birthed as a ministry of faith. God's vision was that of a growing church with people from every walk of life coming from the north, south, east and west. Today, The Day Star Tabernacle International is alive and vibrant with God's Word.

The present location of the church was occupied in May, 1991. The 17.63 acres of the campground includes: The Sanctuary, The Family Life Center, The Sonshine Gymnasium, The Courts of Praise Tennis Courts, The Agape Place, The Fun Zone and our new Home of the Saints Softball field and picnic area. There are currently 45 ministries in place for the edifying and building up of those inside and outside the Body of Christ.

The current sanctuary houses our Stars of Heaven Children's Nursery and is the campus site of the Christian Life School of Theology.

We are a body of people who believe we should carry God's Word and share it with others. God's message is carried on the airwaves with "The Brightness of His Glory" weekly radio broadcast. The "Lion of Judah" television ministry is seen all over the United States and broadcasts on the Inspirational

Network Worldwide.

The Lord has blessed us with a corporate anointing for traveling to minister to various churches nationally and internationally as God leads.

We have a ministry of an evangelistic thrust reaching communities, prisons and hospitals. We are a body of believers that are excited and jubilant about worshipping and praising God with an intense enthusiasm.

Dr. Horton travels the globe ministering on prophecy and eschatology. God has placed an anointing on him to proclaim and teach about end-times from the book of Revelation and to equip the Body of Christ to "see beyond what we see". Dr. Horton has a prophetic ministry in teaching other books of the Bible, allowing the Body of Christ to understand the Spirit of Wisdom and the revelation in the knowledge of Him (Jesus Christ). Apostle Horton has written two other books, *God's Numbers and What They Mean* and *Oh! How the Days are Telling.*

The Day Star Tabernacle International is in covenant relationship with over 600 other ministries throughout the world including India, Africa, Mexico and the Philippines. Dr. Horton and his wife, Alicia, reside in Douglasville, GA, a suburb west of Metro Atlanta.

"Therefore the redeemed of the Lord shall return, and come with singing unto Zion; and everlasting joy shall be upon their head: they shall obtain gladness and joy; and sorrow and mourning shall flee away."
Isaiah 51:11

ACKNOWLEDGMENTS

Thanks to my lovely wife, Elder Alicia Horton, for always holding a standard and encouraging me in the work of the Lord.

Thanks to Sister Sherion Harris and Mother Mary Carter for gathering all the materials of Apostle's work. To Elder Robin Cooke, Deaconess Lorvina Cooke, Sister Alicia Bonner and Sister Dinah Robinson for working to edit and complete the book.

Let the redeemed say so,

Dr. H. L. Horton, Apostle

"...for He taught them as one that had authority, and not as the scribes."
Mark 1:22

DEDICATION

This book is dedicated to the men and women who are soldiers in the army of the Lord-who resist the adversary steadfast in the faith. For the Word is nigh thee, even in thy mouth.

To my wife Elder Alicia Horton and The Day Star Tabernacle International Family, continue to "Speak Life Only" in your victorious walk with the Lord. As always, pray without ceasing because prayer changes ALL things.

"Let the words of my mouth, and the meditation of my heart, be acceptable in thy sight, O Lord, my strength and my redeemer."
Psalm 19:14

"Thou therefore endure hardness, as a good soldier of Jesus Christ. No man that warreth entangleth himself with the affairs of this life; that he may please him who hath chosen him to be a soldier."
2 Timothy 2:3, 4

INTRODUCTION

During the course of the past 18 years, Dr. H. L. Horton, Apostle of The Day Star Tabernacle International, has been preaching the Word of God unashamedly with the passion of a man on fire from heaven's gate world. We have been provoked, enlightened and loved by his words of encouragement and spiritual insight behind the veil of the flesh. Apostle Horton's words of wisdom have always caused us to put our thinking caps on and *"bring our brains to church"*. He has brought us from the backward spaces of our earthly passions to realizing God's plan for our lives and seeing through *"dove eyes"*.

If we've learned nothing else over the years, it's that Apostle Horton is a man after God's own heart and sincerely desires to impart wisdom and understanding into God's people. To this end, we have collected an assortment of the hundreds of *"phrases that preach"* that we have been blessed to receive from the Man of God.

Often as you read through this literature, you will be tempted to simply gloss by many of the profound sayings that have come from the throne room, that so eloquently express His intent. Be forewarned, put on your thinking cap and spiritual eyeglasses, then take your time to discover these beautiful phrases of life-changing wisdom. Only then will you discover what we at The Day Star Tabernacle International have learned; that God can and does use his prophets to speak to the Body of Christ.

By no means are these all the collective words of wisdom, but merely those we recorded, remembered or heeded. Many of these phrases are stand-alone messages in that they can preach a complete sermon by themselves, but we only encourage this one thing, use each as a learning tool to draw you nearer to the Word of God that you may be doers and not hearers only. You will no longer desire to be associated with faith-robbing phrases.

...It's What You Keep Saying
By Dr. H. L. "Skip" Horton

Chapter 1
RENEW YOUR MIND . . .
Ephesians 4:23 "And be renewed in the Spirit of your mind. And that ye put on the new man, which after God is created in righteousness and true holiness."

1. If you always do what you've always done, you'll always get what you've always got.

2. Comparison kills contentment.

3. You can make it, if you can take it.

4. God only sees two men on the planet, Adam and Jesus - And we are in one or the other.

5. There is a thinker behind the thoughts.
   Think like the thinker of the thoughts.

6. WIN = What's Important Now

7. Purpose keeps you focused.

8. Stop feeding your new man, old man thoughts!

9. Your life is never going to be more exciting than you are.

10. Who you be, is not what you do!

11. You frame your world with your words.

12. Jesus is the solution for all your pollution.

13. When you say impossible, God says I am possible!

14. The battle of faith is fought in the mind.

15. Bitterness produces bitterness.

16. When dreams are shattered, you must decide to conquer rather than be conquered.

17. Attitude determines altitude!

18. Worry is assuming God's responsibility.

19. Do the thing you fear the most, and the death of that fear is certain.

20. You cannot give away what someone will not receive.

21. A lazy person is never happy.

22. It is not until we are broken of our pride, that God is then free to flow out of us.

23. Obedience is better than sacrifice.

24.   Begin to "Per dict your mint", how much I want, not how much I got.

25.   Speak Life Only!

26.   When you fool down, begin to speak the Word to change your mind.

27.   Get into the Word and the Word will get into you!

28.   I Think! I Want! I Feel! - Soulish components

29.   God works from the head down, not the body up.

30.   F. E. A. R. = False Evidence Appearing Real

31.   Condemnation is destructive, conviction is constructive.

32.   Oppression is anger turned inwardly.

33.   Christians experience convictions, sinners experience condemnation.

34.   Pity leads to condemnation.

35.   God can make nothing, something!

36.   God does not give you fear, He gives you faith!

37.   If you want to change your life, change your

Words.

38. Don't get frustrated between the "revelation" of the dream, and the "manifestation" of the dream!

39. Abuse is abnormal use.

40. Jesus comes where He is celebrated, not tolerated.

41. You must speak the Word of God, to give God space to bring it about in your life.

42. We must go through the cross experience.

43. Turn your attention to God and God will turn His attention to you!

44. You've got to get up off your bottom so you can get to the top!

45. Lose "your" mind and put on the mind of Christ!

46. Don't take the less because you made a mistake!

47. Thoughts outside the thoughts of God are illegal and misleading!
God is the only legitimate originator of all thoughts.

48. The Holy Spirit is the only legitimate initiator of those thoughts.

49. Are you a product of a cross less gospel?

50. Lust is always consuming, but never satisfied.

51. You get what you use. A measure of faith!

52. God is always speaking. Do we hear? Do we obey?

53. Without mistakes, there can be no progress.

54. You look just like your decisions.

55. God does not move by your tears, but by His Word.

56. There is a knowledge above college.

57. F.A.I.T.H. Forsaking All I Trust Him.

58. Fear is the opposite of Faith.

59. Before we go up, we must grow up!

60. E.G.O. Edging God Out.

61. Stop killing today with yesterday.

62. Supernatural assistance for supernatural existence.

63. Declaring God's strength!

64. Each new day is a miracle in progress.

65. Faith is an anchor.

66. Stay in the zone of confidence.

67. Do the Word of God – not your feelings.

68. There are no failures; we simply did it the wrong way.

69. Re-prioritize your priorities.

70. The will of God is escorted to earth by prayer.

71. We walk NOT in the limited, but the unlimited.

72. Ignorance is healed by knowledge.

73. Success is your being what God called you to be (do).

74. Prayer should replace faultfinding.

75. The devil's success depends upon your ignorance.

76. Jesus died as you – not instead of you!

77. Every word carries a spirit.

78. Words can make you or break you.

79.   The Cross is God's way of removing your old man!

80.   Lust does not sleep.

81.   You have no options, you are a servant.

82.   Your nature is who you are.

83.   The old man does not exist if you are born again.

84.   You will have what you Think!

85.   Crown of thorns = cursed thinking.

86.   There is power in consecration.

87.   God gives vision - not division.

88.   Born-A-Gain = You were born to gain - not to lose.

89.   God receives pleasure when things are in order.

90.   Wisdom is applying the finished work to your present life.

91.   If you can perceive it, you can hold it in your hand.
       The key to success in the Lord is to get into His plan.

92. We are City Reachers and Nation Takers.

93. Your tongue is a launching pad.

94. Don't let your ear end up being a trash can.

95. Words that emanate from the flesh cannot justify.

96. The devil lives (operates) by the power of suggestions; the Lord lives (operates) by "IT IS WRITTEN." Your thought process is already perceived by God.

97. Where there is a problem, you need to sow a seed.

98. God permits tests in your life.

99. Pictures are the language of the Spirit.

100. Get your mind out of the world; get your Bible off the shelf.

101. People see you as you think you are!

102. Before you become something, you have to see something.

103. Words are thoughts, and thoughts are things.

104. Live by what you don't see (faith).

105. Pride = overestimating yourself and under-estimating others.

106. It's time to declare war on stupidity!

107. Your imagination should be harnessed by the Word of God.

108. You are the product of what you've said all your life.

109. Change your world by changing your words.

110. You should have a doorkeeper over your mouth.

111. You Get What You Say!!

112. If you fear the Lord, you would not talk negatively. (You see what you say!)

113. The battle is in the mind.

114. You can be benefited by right thinking.

115. Memorial = created to remind you of something.

116. Where the focus goes, the power flows.

117. Revelation knowledge goes past the halls of your senses right into your spirit.

118. You are free by the truth you know.

119. Your carnal mind is blocking the visibility of Jesus.

120. You can speak life or death into your situation.

121. Stop thinking that you are a discontinued product.
      You will get out of layaway soon!

122. Stop failing and start prevailing!

123. Your circumstances don't make who you are.

124. Thoughts are unborn words.

125. Problems are never worries until you chronically think about them.

126. All problems are in the soul (mind).

127. A man cannot live above his thoughts.

128. You get what you think. You are on the same step as your thoughts. You can go No higher than your thoughts.

129. We spend all of our time trying to get rid of who we used to be, instead of enjoying who we are.

130. Your life is a warning or an example.

131.   Bring your brain to Church.

132.   Christianity is not your responsibility, but your response to God's ability.

133.   Jesus is the head of who we are. He died as who we used to be, and came out as who we are today.

134.   We know, we know who we are!

135.   If you don't know the truth, thoughts will wear you out.

136.   When you look back, it holds you back.

137.   It is illegal to park in unforgiveness.

138.   Don't let your situation intimidate you.

139.   People who are broken are masters at mending.

140.   Life is not always fair, but God is always there.

141.   God is a predestined God, so He finishes the end - - before He starts the beginning.

142.   Sin is not an act, it is a nature-that causes an act.

143.   The trip to Calvary is a one-way ticket – you don't come back, you died with Christ.

144.   You need to see the removal of your old man.

Chapter 2
PROVERBIAL TIDBITS . . .
Isaiah 26:3 "Thou wilt keep him in perfect peace, whose mind is stayed on the: because he trusteth in thee."

1. B.I.B.L.E. Basic Instructions Before Leaving Earth

2. God has no respect of person, but does have respect of principles.

3. Jesus Class is better than First Class.

4. Let the mind of the Master, be the Master of your mind.

5. God's going to shake you until He wakes you!

6. You need insight before you have outsight. (If you can see it on the inside, you can have it on the outside).

7. God will stretch you like a rubber band.

8. Put some feet to your faith.

9. Say it until you see it.

10. Satan's favorite point of entry is from your love ones, people who are closest to you.

11.   Satan always tries to bring corruption into creativity.

12.   All or not at all!

13.   Pigeons flop, but eagles fly!

14.   Average is on top of the bottom.

15.   When you trust in yourself, you walk in deception.

16.   Making the Vision Visible!

17.   Follow the cloud and not the crowd!

18.   What's the good of winning in public and losing in private?

19.   The church is no stronger than the "churches" that's in it.

20.   Brokenness produces progress—if your heart is right with God.

21.   Reactions will make you or break you.

22.   God is more interested in your character than your comfort.

23.   You are only as sick as your secrets!

24. Suffering is a necessity for glorification.

25. Speak what is well of each other.

26. Love is God, because God is love!

27. You can have as many degrees as a thermostat and still burst hell wide open!

28. Get in your set place and be connected.

29. When you start wrong, you end up wrong.

30. You can't give pearls to people who like costume jewelry.

31. Love will keep your fire burning.

32. When the devil comes, don't react – respond.

33. We have been purchased with a price.

34. It is not enough to know the Word, you must become the Word!

35. Love is the essence of the gospel.

36. Death equalizes everyone, rich or poor.

37. Who is Jesus to you?

38. Patience has no place in quicksand.

39.   We must have a willingness to please God.

40.   Knowledge = Know the Ledge;   Understand = Who's under your standing?

41.   Everything that is good is not easy.

42.   Love can abound in knowledge and in judgment.

43.   Make your will the WILL of God.

44.   Fear (healthy) the Lord, and He will control you.

45.   God has the last decision.

46.   The top influences the bottom.

47.   Spirit is thicker than blood.

48.   God calls us and equips us.

49.   Christ is the lawgiver and the lawkeeper.

50.   Where there is a thigh, there is strength.

51.   The seed is the Word of God.

52.   Self-love is struggling for recognition.

53.   The earth (world) will never end! The world's system will end.

54. Satan's system puts a premium on education; God is for edification.

55. If you don't walk in the will of God, you will walk in the will of the devil.

56. Jewels are refined under pressure.
Saints that can't take anything are like costume jewelry.

57. Cross = Your will crosses the will of God.

58. We live in a relative world, but God is absolute.

59. God of the plenty work with the many.

60. Most people want God to be a Savior, but not Lord!

61. The anointing is the ability to get the work done.

62. The seed within gives the fruits without.

63. Sin is choosing self over God!

64. The Body of Christ is an organism – not an organization.

65. The flesh is an unproductive commodity.

66. Stop trying to get your answers from the devil's system.

67.   Fruits are what develops us; Works are what God develops through us.
FRUITS   =   Character; God is looking for character.

68.   You cannot trust the urges that come from the flesh.

69.   God is only impressed with Jesus.

70.   Jesus has passed the exam and put the results in your file (The Bible). Walk in the results!

71.   The fit man took the old man away. (Fit man = Jesus Christ)

72.   The main thing is to keep the main thing the main thing!

73.   The church is not a good idea, but a God idea.

74.   Proclamation is to get you saved; Explanation will mature you.

75.   GOSPEL = Good News; Good – because we need it; News = because it has already happened - Prophecy.

76.   There is not a sin problem, but there is a sinner problem.

77.   SOUL = who you are; your uniqueness in God.

78. Imagination = Image and Nation (a nation of images) They will take you!!

79. Sin has a form of insanity to it.

80. The Bible will keep you from sin, but sin will keep you from the Bible.

81. Laugh at the devil, it throws him off.

82. Redeemed words build Jesus up, while natural words build up self.

83. Words from heaven will bring SELF to light.

84. Redeemed talk will divide the natural from the spiritual and the inward from the outward.

85. The potential is in the Seed.

86. Sin is active; it moves.

87. M.E.D.I.A. = Many Evil Doers In Action

88. A cup is a container. God is into filling and pouring.

89. God is revealing what He has already done.

90. OF = Originated From; source

91. The love of God brings satisfaction, not natural

love.

92.   Natural love is a fallen thing.

93.   Self-preservation is the first law of selfishness, the preservation of others is the law of love.

94.   Love embraces truth.

95.   Grace is love in manifestation.

96.   Prophecy = Pre-revealed Knowledge.

97.   Things are not pathetic – but prophetic.

98.   Name means nature.

99.   Spirits do not die!! God is a spirit.

100. We are new because Jesus is new. When Jesus was resurrected, He was made new.

101. Lukewarm = not understanding who you are!

102. The Holy Spirit is not a WHAT but a WHOM!

103. The Promised Land is a Promised Man!

104. Sin is being independent of God.

105. DOOR = His appearing; County seat = your heart.

106. WHEAT = death; BARLEY = eternal life (resurrection), bread of life.

107. Jesus died on the cross, but you fell through the gate.

108. Olive Oil = anointing of God.

109. God is satisfied with the finished work of Jesus Christ.

110. ACTS = Adoration, Confession, Thanksgiving, Supplication

111. Promise = JESUS!

112. The Word of God is like an unlimited superman.

113. Religion = the greatest friend of the devil and the greatest enemy of the Lord!

114. Check your mouth (words)!

115. MIRROR = WORD

116. Obtaining a good report is saying what God says about a thing.

117. Dismayed = deprived of the ability to act.

118. Put the Word to work. It does it all.

119. No training; no reigning.

120. Jesus saves and God gets the glory.

121. Peace is a person. PEACE is Jesus!

122. Choice = a combination of words that you decided to speak to work for you. Your reality is inside of you.
The Word of God needs to be within because it won't return void. God's Word is good pleasure.

123. Eternity is already set in your heart.

124. The beginning and end is a person (Jesus), not a definition.

125. Patterns = Cycles of truth.

126. MOAB = Land of curses.

127. The Lord is in the IS!

128. Correction is for protection.

129. There is a place in faith called UNITY!

130. Tradition invalidates the Word of God.

131. Deception = a lie believed to be the truth; lie = a falsehood.

132. Brick = man-made idea; Stone = eternal truth

133. God drew us into His purpose.

134. Obedience to the Word of God is NEVER a risk.

135. Spirits can persuade. They have NO gender.

136. You can't be like Jesus. Only Jesus can be like Jesus, in you.

137. You can't act like the devil unless the devil is in you.

138. "A tradition" = 666

139. Christianity is not a do-good religion.

140. God is not impressed with your gifts. He wants fruits.

141. Infirmities = our inability to produce results because of the limitations imposed on us by the flesh.

142. Your flesh is not you. It is the container (vessel) that houses your spirit.

143. God was around before start got started, before begin begun!

144. Behave = you be, you have!

145. Sin = Missing the mark!

146. Bible = a book of "reversals".

147. You don't know what's in the tea bag until you put it in hot water.

148. We don't give the imitator more glory than the originator.

149. John the Baptist ministry is coming back!

150. Anybody who is not saved today, his life is a lie.

151. As we come into the Tribulation Period, don't run from "authority".

152. The strength of your position is knowing, and it is a knowing that will throw or thrust you beyond your five senses.

153. Love is an iron fist inside of a velvet glove.

154. People with character do something with what they have learned.

155. Perseverance will outlast persecution.

156. Scalpture retractions is frowning.

157. Covenant is commitment.

158. A little sin will do you in.

159. Concern is a renegade cell that keeps multiplying.

160. What's up? Jesus!

161. Stop being naughty by nature.

162. Get ready for the gospel flight.

163. Small people draw small circles to keep people out. Wise people draw large circles to include everybody.

164. People have no wisdom now, because they have no fear.

165. We have become obsessed with our own significance.

166. No Hope = don't know the Lord
Blessed Hope = know the Lord

167. Be ready, Not get ready!

168. Obedience's passion is rewards; Love's passion is oneness!

169. Mistakes should be stepping stones to something great.

170. You give the devil worship when you walk in condemnation!

171. The Church is just a mindset so that we can know about the Kingdom of God!

172. You shouldn't retire, you should finish!

173. Concept = man's ideas about something from a fallen state!

174. Attract abundance by living upright!

175. We are not a "we be not". We are a "we be able"!

176. God reveals what He wants to heal!

177. Revelation of the Word of God brings relationship!

178. God's words are eternal; man's words are temporal!

179. Understanding = backing back up the road of start to see how you finish!

180. We need supernatural eyesight to give us supernatural insight!

181. I can be raised by the power of praise!

182. If you keep your praise on, you will never step

out of pocket!

183. God, thanks for waking us up this morning and starting us on Your way!

184. If you be willing, you will eat of the fat of the land!

185. Some things are permitted into our lives as tutors and teachers to help us understand the will of God.

186. God doesn't want "wimpy" Christians!

187. Are you in the willful pursuit of the practice of sin?

188. If you are living in the flesh, you are wasting your life!

189. Jesus is The Master Builder in a human junk yard.

190. The outcome of right doctrine is love.

191. We can do this one or two ways: God's way or God's way!

192. God lives at the intersection of Praise and Thanksgiving Blvd!
Worship is His P.O.Box!

193. The enemy does not fear the church, because the church does not fear the Lord.

194. Extending the boundaries of grace can turn into disgrace!

195. We are not in competition, we are in completion - - of each other!

196. God is turning the pages of history, and we are about to get to the back of the book (Bible).

197. Whatsoever is in the vine ought to be seen in the branches!

198. The key to passing over is to eat more lamb!

199. You can't go wrong with right!

200. The devil has no satisfied customers!

201. I can do all things in Him, who is my ability and strength!

202. The Rules of Life are already set by the Life-Giver!

203. Afflict your soul and walk in the finished work!

204. It's not an outfit, it's an infit!

205. As a man thinketh, so is he!

206. You got to stay under the canopy of faith!

207. Self-efforts cut the blessings of God!

208. The church is designed to create a kingdom of Priests!

209. The testimony of Jesus is the Spirit of Prophecy!

210. PHD: Praise Him Daily!

211. The eyes of man are never satisfied!

212. Jesus is the lover of your soul!

213. God can do for you what no other god can do!

214. Good folks don't go to heaven, you must be born again to be connected to God!

215. Vision is the ability to see further than you can look!

216. Seeing it, before you see it.

217. Every opposition is an opportunity!

218. There's truth in your Spirit that your head isn't completely aware of yet.

219. When you come to your end, God begins.

220. God is not blessing your flesh, but your Spirit.

221. Don't box God in.

222. You can't receive anything that you are not like.

223. Two streams that are flowing:
(1) Righteousness (2) Sin.

224. Be on a sure footing (foundation).

225. Two factors that will get us through:
(1) prayer (2) obedience.

226. Be quick to repent (genuine repentance).

227. Proverbs is the book of sanctified common sense.

Chapter 3

ABUNDANT LIVING . . .

Isaiah 58:11 "And the Lord shall guide thee continuously, and satisfy thy soul in drought, and make fat thy bones: and thou shalt be like a watered garden, and like a spring of water, whose waters fail not."

1. The Christian life is not a problem free life; it is a carefree life!

2. Who are you in your downtime?

3. Pressure = pre sure (before sure)

4. Don't run to the phone, run to the throne!

5. Your setback is a setup for a comeback.

6. The secret of your future is hidden in your daily routine.

7. Will a man rob God? Robbery means the intent to do harm to the body of Christ.

8. God never consults our past to determine our future.
    When God wants to bless you, He will put someone in your life.
    When satan wants to destroy you, he will put someone in your life.

9.   Integrity is to do the right thing when no one is looking.

10.   What you walk away from will determine what God brings in your life.

11.   Whose body are you in, the body of sin or the body of Christ?

12.   You will see what you say! See what I'm saying?

13.   Have you learned to make a living or have you learned to live?

14.   If God gives you a dream, He has a way to finance it.

15.   When Christ comes in, He brings confidence to face tomorrow.

16.   It is not the past performance, but the present direction that makes you successful with God.

17.   Don't let your prosperity cloud your mind.

18.   In your pressing, there is some blessings.

19.   Are you a "got to have it" Saint?

20.   Go to work on Monday morning with a "high" over!

21.   When you praise you get a raise!

22.   It is not what you "do" for God, it's what you "be" for God!

23.   The devil will come against you, when you're weak and in the wilderness.

24.   Your provision is in the vision!

25.   Time unfolds what eternity has already told.

26.   When the Word enters, understanding comes. Don't let circumstances put your fire out!

27.   God gives you grace for the place!

28.   Mistakes are stepping-stones to something great!

29.   The purpose of adversity is to help our flesh adjust.

30.   Walking outside the Word is where adversity lives.

31.   The real family is the Family of God.

32.   Treasures for your troubles!

33.   W. A. R. = Willing   Able   Ready

34.   A trumpet denotes "a clear sounding Word".

35 .   **Six Steps** to the throne: Crucified, Dead, Buried, Quickened, Raised and Seated!

36.   Every person has a purpose for being in your life.

37.   Our purpose is connected to someone else's problem.

38.   Our deliverance is connected to someone else's dilemma.

39.   Our miracle is connected to someone else's mess.

40.   God is all about increase.

41.   Don't talk about it, be about it. Witness! Everyday!!

42.   Sometimes when people are talking about you, it draws God's attention to you.

43.   Bloom where you are planted!

44.   Making the impossible, Possible!

45.   Jesus is building the house, and you are just a stone in it.

46.   There is no life outside of Christ, Don't half step with God!

47. The just shall live by faith, not MasterCard or Visa.

48. One person doesn't make up a team.

49. We are a many-membered man.

50. Keep your body under subjection.

51. Every time you listen to the devil, you go down.

52. Glory has a hope - - - Jesus in you, the Hope of Glory!

53. The devil will set you up to mess you up.

54. Each one, reach one!

55. Death brings life!

56. No roots, no fruits!

57. Delayed answers to your prayers mean that God is adding. . .

58. A test usually follows a command.

59. Add to your prayer "giving."

60. Are you really what you are on the outside, hiding what you are on the inside, pretending to be somebody you're really not?

61.   Don't make hasty decisions in a crisis situation.

62.   Be on the attack, and you won't be under attack.

63.   Offenses are designed to collapse your life.

64.   Learn to see beyond what you see.

65.   Familiarity makes you lazy and takes things for granted.

66.   In problems, sling the mantle (Holy Ghost).

67.   Stop seeing people as interruptions in your life.

68.   Praise is oxygen for your spirit.

69.   Faith is to build character.

70.   Failures and trials are the eggs we break to make the omelet of life a success.

71.   Little inconveniences develop your character.

72.   G.R.A.C.E. = God's Riches At Christ's Expense!!

73.   Don't Count God Out!!

74.   Charity is love in action.

75. Teaching will grow you up; preaching will get you saved!

76. If you are rowing the boat, you don't have time to rock it.

77. When the horse is dead, dismount it.

78. Faithfulness is going with the opportunity. Never get complacent.

79. Get involved in the vision so you can receive provision.

80. Efficiency = doing things right; Effectiveness = doing the right thing at the right time. Encouragement is like oxygen to the soul.

81. You learn in the valley, not live in the valley.

82. Failure is the opportunity to use more wisdom next time.

83. Some things you go through are for growth.

84. We don't wear the badge of doubt.

85. The place of sacrifice is the place of fullness.

86. You obey the truth through the Spirit.

87. You get promoted when you pass the test.

88. You pray the provisions, NOT your wants/needs.

89. Seek God, not things!

90. Salvation is free, but you will pay a price for maturity.

91. God tells you who you are, then He shows you how you got to be who you are, so you will believe.

92. Don't major in the minor; circumstances are the minor.

93. Faith is trusting God and waiting to receive.

94. If you don't like your harvest, check your seed!

95. You must "give" to get.

96. If Jesus hadn't died instead of us, that would leave us US!

97. Death is not a final state, it is a condition.

98. It's good to come to church, but it is better to be the church!

99. You are working for God not man!

100. "Give" to get out of debt.

101. God started Finish – Maturity is working your way back to start to see how you finished!

102. Things don't make things; faith does.

103. You give tithes by reason and offerings by revelation.

104. You don't live for yourself, you live for others.

105. Say, "This too shall pass" about your situation.

106. If you favor God's cause (vision), He will multiply you.

107. What's true of Christ is true of you in Him.

108. Persecution is good for you, it brings increase from God!

109. God is taking off of you what the devil has put on you, and He is putting into you what the devil has taken out of you.

110. It's the death that gives life.

111. We think we are "what we did". God has covered this and made us a new man.

112. Belief activates things in your life.

113. In order to get a benefit, you must first have a fit.

114. You pay a high price for low living.

115. Crucifixion is not a way of life, but an event that produces a way of life. That life is the life of Christ!

115. Life is a series of choices.

116. The devil comes in to confuse your understanding.

117. Your daily routine requires choices.

118. There are NO hopeless situations, but only people who give up hope.

119. Hope is like a rope, it pulls out the evidence that you need.

120. Jesus didn't come because you were bad, He came because you were dead in your trespasses and sins.
He came back to bring LIFE!

121. We need to be a people with ears up to the Shepherd's lips.

122. Turning your obstacles into opportunities - supernatural assistance!

123. Jesus was hung up for our "hang-ups"!

124. Obedience is prosperity.

125. Everybody wants to get "a – head". A "head" is Christ Jesus.

126. A backbone will accomplish more than a wishbone.

127. God thinks it, Jesus says it, and the Holy Ghost does it.

128. Words make personality.

129. Worship is an expression of intimacy.

130. Perseverance will always outlast persecution.

131. It's not what God can do for you, but what He can do through you.

132. There is power in agreement.

133. Faith is getting a "grip" on God; Redemption is God getting a grip on you.

134. The devil gives you many life styles, but NOT eternal life.

135. God has a right to discontinue your service if you are delinquent in payment.

136. Money spent on high fashion does not resolve low self-esteem.

137. Your credit rating is synonymous with your character rating.

138. The only difference between debt and the devil is that the devil can't get any bigger.

139. It's not your income but your outcome.

140. Financial healing begins with plastic surgery.

141. God will never put in your hand what is not in your heart.

142. Goals are like eyeglasses; they help give you sight.

143. God left us here to be Covenant establishers.

144. Obedience = boundary lines designed to keep your scoring drive alive.

145. When you lie; you give up reality and live in fantasy.

146. The perfect union is the soul and spirit coming together.

147. Qualify to be multiplied is to obey the Word.

148. When you murmur and complain, you set yourself up for the destroyer.

149. Teaching is not beneficial to you until you choose right thinking.

150. Right thinking is understanding what influences you

151. Two wings: In order to overcome, you must (1) surrender, (2) trust.

152. The purpose of your need is to make you into Somebody.

153. Keys of the kingdom: (1) death, (2) burial, (3) resurrection.

154. You have NO past life of Adam!!

155. We are growing up into an understanding.

156. In order to receive, you must be a receptor.

157. God blesses obedience.

158. Money doesn't make character.

159. Nevertheless = Never the less! Never take the less.

160. The higher you fly, the better your perspective.

161. Zeal = intense enthusiasm

162. Education refines your five senses; edification builds up your Spirit.

163. Prayer is an attitude of advancement, communication with God.

164. The level of your expectation determines how much you have.

165. God is in your tomorrow.

166. Things don't give increase. God does!

167. The invisible makes the visible.

168. Give with expectation.

169. God can step into your destiny and rearrange your future!

170. Unforgiveness stops miracles and blessings!

171. Adversity is the catalyst for fruit.

172. LIVE = Live in Vertical Expectation – Keep looking up!

173. It's not what you are going through but what you are going to.

174. We are just passengers in the vehicle of the will of God.

175. Your flesh will send you to hell and won't even show up!

176. God didn't call you to try, He called you to die!

177. Can you watch me change clothes without being offended?

178. Secret sins are setting you up for a defeat.

179. Keep the word of God in your mouth!

180. Jesus is building the Father a house, which house you are. That's why He came as a Carpenter.

181. Know the Word, and become what you know.

182. Church is a vehicle to stretch you.

183. It is time to operate in humility.

184. You are going to get what is purposed to you.

185. True prosperity is being in the will of God.

186. If you are not dead to trespasses and sins, you ought to be scared.

187. Doorway of your opportunity is disguised in your opposition.

188. According to the Redemption Plan, God is a God of a new beginning, not a second chance.

189. We are living in the generation that will see Jesus!

190. God is the ultimate bookkeeper. He believes in accountability.

191. Walk with Kings, but keep the common touch.

192. Procrastination is disobedience in slow motion.

193. If you buy the lie, you will live the lie.

194. Successful people do daily what unsuccessful folks won't do.

195. It is good to be in the House of God, but it is better to be the House of God.

196. Get submitted to somebody so shame and poverty don't follow you.

197. If you hear and regard instructions, honor will come into your life.

198. Are you sitting around on the stool of do nothing?

199. Lazy people don't think well.

200. God is shaking us from our dreams and awaking us to His vision.

201. Problems come from ignoring past promptings of the Holy Spirit.

202. Everyday is not going to be a good day, but a GOD day!

203. In order to fellowship, you must first have relationship.

204. . . . for even Christ pleased not himself.

205. The end result is not a visitation, but a habitation!

206. If you don't know your titles, you don't know your rights.

207. Your attitude can be an idol.

208. Prayer is designed for personal relationship. For intimacy.

209. All in Adam seek life which leads to death, All in Christ seek death which leads to life.

210. Affliction lets you feel who you used to be, so you can appreciate who you are now.

211. Some are plugged in and some are attached.

212.   Dressed up, but messed up!

213.   You got to know your purpose to find out what your limitations are!

214.   When God is in front, He leads. When God is alongside, He comforts. When God is behind, He's got your back!

215.   A betrayer is someone who is never with you.

216.   Discouraged = no courage!

217.   Nothing in life becomes dynamic until you become specific.

218.   Every tub has to sit on its own bottom!

219.   When Adam fell, we started slipping into darkness!

220.   You will never see a U-haul behind a Hurst.

221.   You don't have it made until you make it to the end!

222.   Jesus died your death, so you can live His life!

223.   Secret sins are setting you up for a defeat.

224.   Good, Better, Best; never let it rest; until your good is better and your better is best!

225. Know the Word and become what you know!

226. The end of your Faith, is the Salvation of your Soul.

227. Don't be a legalistic tithor, but be a cheerful giver.

228. Watch wasted finances on Ishmael (flesh).

229. Don't get stuck in past hurts and disappointments.

230. Living comes to an end, but life does not.

231. We'll never be comfortable until we get to heaven.

232. The beast nature produces the kingdom of self.

233. Don't let your emotions cloud your sound judgment.

234. People don't hear what you say, they hear what you keep saying.

235. We know about sonship, but don't know the Spirit of the Son.

236. Jesus is looking for some Millennium thinkers.

237. Heard, but not heeding.

238.   Your life will follow your thoughts.

239.   Perfect people are not in the church, they are
       being perfected!

*"... I am come that they might have life, and that
they might have it more abundantly."
John 10:10*